out of the ordinary

Pollard Thomas Edwards architects

Copyright © 2005
Black Dog Publishing Limited and
Pollard Thomas Edwards architects

Black Dog Publishing Limited

Unit 4.4 Tea Building
56 Shoreditch High Street
London
E1 6JJ
Tel: +44 (0)20 7613 1922
Fax: +44 (0)20 7613 1944
Email: info@bdp.demon.co.uk
www.bdpworld.com

Pollard Thomas Edwards architects

Diespeker Wharf
38 Graham Street
London
N1 8JX

Tel: 020 7336 7777
Fax: 020 7336 0770

Merchants Court
Derby Square
Liverpool
L2 1TS

Tel: 0151 703 2220
Fax: 0151 703 2229

www.ptea.co.uk

ISBN 1 904772 34 X

DESIGNED BY
Isambard Thomas

PRINTED IN THE EU

ACKNOWLEDGEMENTS

Alan Powers is a journalist and writer. Stephen Chance is a director of PTEa. Bill Thomas is a former partner and founder of PTEa.

Special thanks to: Roger Pollard, Bill Thomas and John Edwards
Thanks also to: Wendy Ebringer, Patrick LeLarge, Peggy Mead and Paul Simon

PHOTOGRAPHERS
Dennis Gilbert/VIEW 13, 19 [bottom right], 22 [bottom right], 39, 56, 58, 79 [top], 88, 96 [bottom left], 97, 98, 99 [both], 104 [1985], 105 [1988], 106 [1993], 106 [2001], 107 [1995, 1996]: **Paul Tyagi** 16, 69, 70, 72, 73 [bottom], 79 [bottom], 106 [1998], 106 [2000], 107 [1994], 107 [1997]: **Richard Bryant/arcaid.co.uk** 20, 61 [bottom], 104 [1983], 105 [1981]: **Tim Soar** 25: **Jason Orton** 29, 30, 32, 33: **Robert Greshoff** 34, 35, 40, 41 [both], 42, 43, 89, 93, 101: **Peter Strobel** 37, 48, 52, 53 [top], 63: **Edward Hill** 49, 50: **Rupert Truman** 60, 90, 91, 96 [top right], 107 [2003]: **Martin Charles** 61 [top], 104 [1976], 105 [1979, 1980], 106 [1991]: **Edmund Sumner/VIEW** 68 [both], 77 [both], 107 [2005]: **David Churchill** 102 [bottom left], 103: **Horst Kolo** 104 [1982, 1984]: © **Jeremy Cockayne/arcaid.co.uk** 105 [1986], 105 [1989], 106 [1990]: **Peter Cook/VIEW** 105 [1987]: © **Peter Durant /arcblue.com** 106 [1992]: **Clive Armitage** 106 [1999]: **Nathan Willock/ VIEW** 107 [2002]: **Andrea Heselton** 107 [2004]: © **Peter Jeffree/ Architectural Association** 22: © **Celestine Henderson/Architectural Association** 24: © **Frank Gerssen/ Architectural Association** 18

OTHER CREDITS
© **Getmapping plc** Aerial map 10, 28
teammacarie 3-D image 38
Reproduced by permission of London Borough of Lambeth 75
Uniform 3-D image p 94
© **Alan Godfrey Maps** 36, 82
© **Crown Copyright and database right. All rights reserved.** 39, 76, 84, 95, 98

"We are affected by our everyday surroundings. To worry about ordinary places means imagining that happiness might have an unostentatious, unheroic character to it. Architecture, even in its mightiest examples, will only ever be a small, and imperfect protest against the state of things. But it may be that it's when we make ordinary places that our protest is most effective."

ALAIN DE BOTTON
The Special and the Ordinary

[8–9] Mapping the future: across the capital, each pin marks a PTEa project.

10 Regeneration begins at home STEPHEN CHANCE
16 Enjoyable cities ALAN POWERS

26 Rethinking
28 **Jaywick Sands** affordable housing by the sea
34 **Arundel Square** completing a London square
40 **Sefton Park** new penthouses on old tower blocks
44 **St Jude & St Paul's School** living over the classroom

46 Developers
48 **Angel Waterside** repopulating the backwaters
54 **Connaught Gardens** townhouses in the suburbs
56 **Diespeker Wharf** from timber mill to headquarters
62 **City Wharf** canalside regeneration

66 Community
68 **Whitechapel Community Sports Centre** sport for all
74 **Brockwell Park Lido** saving Brixton beach
76 **Grahame Park** planning the new suburbia

80 Repairing the city fabric: some guidelines BILL THOMAS
Edward Woods Neighbourhood

86 Modernity
88 **Terracotta Court** adding texture to the inner city
92 **Crown Wharf Ironworks** forging ahead on the river
96 **Chillingworth Road** delivering an urban renaissance
100 **Spa Central** healthy living in the park
102 **Belvedere Court** mixed-tenure housing in colour

104 Chronology: selected past work
108 Bibliography
109 Project data
111 PTEa practice

Regeneration begins at home

BY STEPHEN CHANCE

"We know everything within the city connects. Nothing possesses a single or exclusive life. The rich and poor pass beside each other, while the extremes of human experience may meet at any moment. This, too, may be a source of inspiration."

PETER ACKROYD
The Life of the City

These three projects designed by Pollard Thomas Edwards architects triggered the regeneration of CIty Road Basin, Regents Canal, Islington, London.

In the famous opening sequence to the Eames's film *Powers of Ten* the camera zooms in, apparently from outer space. Earth appears, the camera's viewpoint enters the stratosphere and continues towards the surface. Countries, cities, roads and buildings appear. The camera closes in on a locality, on an individual and moves right through the surface, under the skin, to the biology within.

In this image all scales are linked in a single trajectory. By extension past, present and future can be connected in the same way. Making an impact on the universe, for an architect, is an almost negligible act, given the scale of things. On the other hand, vast changes such as earthquakes or political movements can start infinitesimally, like a virus, with an idea, or a tiny mutation. At Pollard Thomas Edwards architects (PTEa) we consider that good architecture begins like this: with the needle, not the haystack. This is how our architecture develops, moving upwards and outwards.

Our regeneration of the City Road Basin area in Islington is like this. It started on a domestic scale, with the planting of a community garden; it grew to embrace a whole urban quarter.

The immediate vicinity of PTEa's base at Diespeker Wharf is a kind of living workshop of urban regeneration. Neighbouring council properties, the canal, a listed building, a new residential development, industrial artefacts, canal cottages and gardens are all part of PTEa's ambitious transformation of its own patch. Inspired by the initial vision of Bill Thomas, one of PTEa's founding partners, the practice designed, co-funded and co-developed it all, bringing along with it neighbours, British Waterways, co-developers and council tenants.

This development also demonstrates the principle of putting something contemporary, and markedly different, into an existing context. PTEa's "crystal" building, a glass boat moored

The clearing of industrial debris for the making of a garden was the first move in the regeneration of an urban quarter.

at the basin's edge, hints at the future transformation of the wider basin.

In these City Road Basin projects architectural design and property development are inextricably linked. Our approach to both is consciously inclusive. We try to understand the web of land ownership. Land lies derelict for years unless difficult ownership patterns can be unpicked. Land can't always be acquired, and in any case *tabula rasa* is not PTEa's style. Often adjoining owners can be brought into the frame of activity to mutual benefit. At Angel Waterside, next to Diespeker, we agreed a right to develop with British Waterways, which remains the freeholder. We remain in discussion with owners of all the adjacent land around the basin to discuss the best implementation of our ideas for the regeneration of the whole area.

Complex city land ownership is a product of history, and in cities history has a tendency to merge past and present, as in Jorge Luis Borges' "A New Refutation of Time", where the past is always lurking just below the surface, showing through where it wears thin, shaping the present, and influencing the future.

PTEa's approach to working with existing buildings and places considers what already exists very carefully before removing anything, however ordinary. We respect the patterns of age and we touch existing fabric as lightly as possible, mending visibly where appropriate and seamlessly only where essential, as in sensitive conservation work. In this way our revitalisation of a dilapidated urban quarter remains in contact with what M Christine Boyer called "the city of collective memory".

This idea of collective memory links to the other linchpin of PTEa's method: we always engage with people. Just as we always extend the definition of the site to its adjacent, nearer and wider context, so we always extend the definition of client to the immediate neighbours and general public.

[ABOVE] Run down "ordinary" fabric of the existing city can be a source of richly evocative base material in any transformative regeneration project.

[BELOW] PTEa's meeting room opens up to the ever-changing context of the Regents Canal.

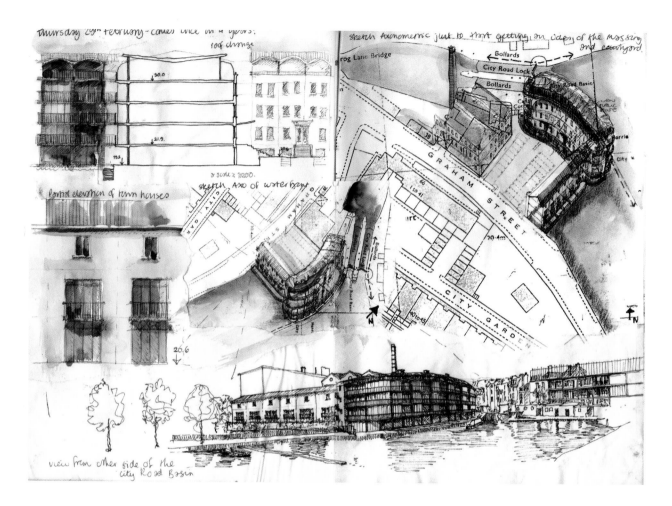

[ABOVE] Early sketches by artist Karen Neale of the existing texture and topography of the neighbourhood.

[RIGHT] Diespeker, Angel Waterside and City Wharf are three components in the regeneration of the waterfront, in which a linear park wraps around the Basin.

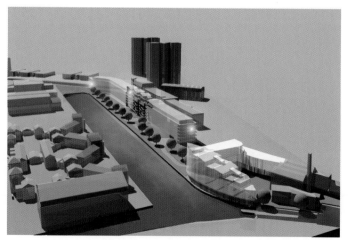

In every new project there is a fount of knowledge that already exists. The people who live and work in an area know more about their neighbourhood than the architect, and a great deal of intellectual capital will have accrued in the area. PTEa works to gain the trust of communities, sometimes alienated and deeply sceptical ones with years of unfulfilled promises and unrealised dreams behind them. Establishing this trust can create value in the social, economic and aesthetic spheres.

In the next phase of the City Road Basin regeneration PTEa has designed, at City Wharf, a mixed-use and mixed-tenure residential development. It includes affordable, key-worker and for-sale housing together with business space and a publicly accessible canalside garden.

I have used the City Road Basin neighbourhood project to say a few things about Pollard Thomas Edwards architects' design approach. This book shows a selection of our most recent projects, some complete and many still under construction. All draw upon the specifics of their location. As Peter Ackroyd notes: "everything within the City connects", and this, for us, is a source of inspiration.

The hanging gardens of the leaf shaped roof of Angel Waterside step right down to the lockside.

Enjoyable cities

BY ALAN POWERS

"Why not exploit and redevelop properties that are in the public domain, vanished streets, lost rivers."

IAIN SINCLAIR
Lights Out for the Territory

The courtyard of PTEa's Angel Waterside
project beside Islington Lock, Regents Canal.

Long before "brownfield site" became a common phrase, indeed, since their foundation in 1974, Pollard Thomas Edwards architects (PTEa) has been guided by concepts of urbanism and high density that are now touchstones of current architectural thinking. PTEa's work shows how it combines modesty with radicalism in an architectural world where there often seems little alternative to either a humdrum performance or a "landmark" that exaggerates its own importance. Current projects include a new school with key-worker flats built over the classroom block and a proposal for decking over the North London railway line to complete a London square. At City Road Basin, one can see how the toehold it first made with its own offices in a converted industrial building was the starting point for creating a new character in the area, adding new to old.

From its early work for housing associations PTEa had already found an architectural

[RIGHT] Waldsiedlung, Berlin by Bruno Taut 1931 (fig 1).
photo © Architectural Association Library

approach that worked for these clients. Over the years, when one would spot in passing an awkward gap site that was being filled in, possibly involving a refurbishment of something already existing, the practice's name would be the one on the red RIBA board. When finished, it would be a building complex that one could look at every time with pleasure. There was a price to be paid for the politeness of these early projects in terms of fame, and as Giles Worsley has written, "Pollard Thomas Edwards... is not one of those architectural practices that craves publicity. It does not go in for high-profile art galleries or buildings with baffling curves and fancy angles that look good in photographs."

The work of PTEa was nearly all in London, and with this seemed to come a special understanding of local "style". To show so much regional sensitivity could be seen as a deviation from the true faith of Modernism. There is a connection, however, between the London builders' vernacular of the eighteenth century and the Modern Movement. During the 1920s and 30s, visiting architects from the continent, such as Bruno Taut, recognised that what they were trying to do in modern architecture was in fact very similar to what the London builders had done a hundred or more years before (fig 1). Taut wrote in 1930 that the old streets and squares were "characterised by wonderful calm and simplicity, with their smooth frontages, plain large windows, etc. (fig 2). They are imbued with the spirit that we should like the new movement to express. There is no trace here of the sentimental, pretty effect with which so many English architects of the present day send their clients into transports."

Ernö Goldfinger, who came from Hungary via Paris, was another outsider who appreciated the strengths of the culture he was entering. His terrace of three houses in Willow Road, Hampstead, completed in 1939, and now

well-known since the largest, Goldfinger's own house, belongs to the National Trust, is an example of the adaptation of Modernism to the spirit of London (fig 3). He chose the terrace form for this site after rejecting an earlier scheme for a free-standing block of flats with no relation to the line of the street. His brick facings and small as well as large windows, are further indications of an inherent relationship between London and the language of Modernism. His terrace deserves a place in an as-yet-unwritten story about how London has accommodated Modern architecture, and vice-versa. Goldfinger even projected how the same house type could be extended from a short terrace into an urban square.

In its sensitivity to various kinds of London typology, PTEa can claim the most respectable Modernist ancestry, for Taut's comment forces us to rethink the received idea that what is traditional is necessarily opposed to what is modern. PTEa has nearly always used brick and used it in ways that produce the kind of lightness and delicacy favoured in the 1930s, unlike much other brick design since the 1970s (fig 4).

The habitual criteria for Modernism in architecture are artistic freedom for innovation and the expression of technological imperatives. Seeing through Taut's eyes, we may understand how, the kind of architecture practised by PTEa is not for that reason marginal to some fundamental principles of Modernism, particularly the social and urban mission that went so wrong when architects during the 1960s thought more about peer group opinion than the views of the users. As a culture, we have learnt that while innovation is certainly needed in housing, the form it takes need not be obviously 'Modern', but may instead simply involve just allowing people to live decently and sustainably rather than heroically. While a large

[ABOVE LEFT] Woodbridge estate. Eighteenth century vernacular – restored by PTEa 1977 (fig 2).

[LEFT] Willow Road, Hampstead by Ernö Goldfinger 1939 (fig 3).

[BELOW LEFT] Goldhawk Road by PTEa 1989 (fig 4).

New Concordia Wharf. PTEa restoration 1984
– "a benchmark in the history of Docklands"
(fig 5).

number of British architects were working
through the precepts of the Athens Charter and
other documents of pre-war thinking, based on
the abolition of the hated "corridor street" and
opening up to fast-moving traffic, theorists
such as Gordon Cullen and Jane Jacobs were
talking about what it feels like to be on the
ground. PTEa never seems to have doubted that
housing could open itself out to the world
rather than turning inwards, yet so disastrous
was the condition of most British cities in the
early 1970s that it would have been hard to
foresee our present achievement of a near-
European lifestyle as a matter of course.

The classic theory of modernism, while
often defective in its understanding of end
users, equally took no account of how the
architect would interact with the world of
money and property. In the writings of Reyner
Banham, a critic who aspired to understand the
modern world in its totality, you don't hear
about architects acting as entrepreneurs, but

today one cannot think of them without
acknowledging their creative role in putting
together collaborative teams of developers,
charities and agencies. Many of the faults of the
1960s might have been avoided if the links
between finance, supply and end-user had
been closer, as they need to be in a more
market-driven society. The nature of
commissions and the way they come to fruition
has changed a lot over the years. The client
seldom simply walks in with a brief and a site
any more. Indeed, people outside the world of
architecture may be surprised at the extent to
which the architect today creates his or her own
job opportunities. Many of these involve pieces
of land with difficulties of ownership that have
left them empty and unused for years.
Commonsense and a concern for the well-
being of the city would indicate that these
Dickensian problems should be solved, and the
government's drive for the redevelopment of
brownfield land adds a further incentive.

Following the change in the architects' Code of Conduct in 1981 which allowed architects to become directly involved in development, PTEa was among the first to take advantage of the new freedom, combining whole or part involvement in the financial aspects of development on some projects with the provision of normal architectural services on others. This continues to be the case, as demonstrated at its own offices, in Diespeker Wharf, a building which was acquired by founding partner Bill Thomas in 1994 from British Waterways. It belongs to a succession of waterside developments it has done, going back to the Anchor Brewhouse, 1989, by Tower Bridge, and New Concordia Wharf, 1984, in Mill Street, Bermondsey, which was described by Stephanie Williams in her book Docklands, 1990, as "a benchmark in the history of Docklands" (fig 5). Diespeker Wharf and Angel Waterside together consist partly of a refurbishment, housing the firm's offices, and an extension along the waterfront in the form of two contrasting ranges of apartments for sale, keeping something of the warehouse aesthetic of plain wall surfaces and repetitive openings, but adding drama with an eye-catching roof profile.

Residential work remains a core activity of the practice, and in this field the difference between public and private may still be crucial in many ways. However it is ceasing, not a moment too soon, to be part of the language of architecture and building. One can immediately conjure images of older Peabody Estates and know that this was "do-good" housing (fig 6). The assumption that public or charitable housing must appear as a world

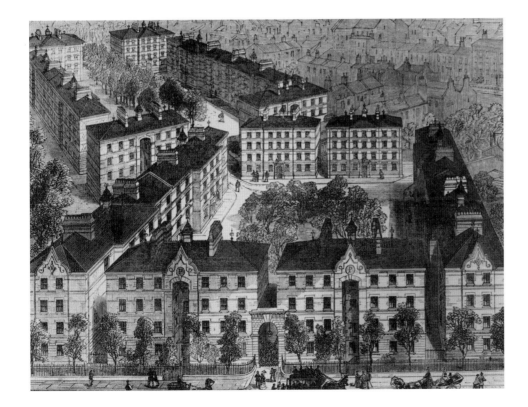

Charity housing c. 1850: the model buildings in Peabody Square, Blackfriars Road, London. Built by the American philanthropist George Peabody as "working men's tenements" for the poor (fig 6).
photo © Getty images

21

apart from the ordinary street goes right back to the beginnings of "housing" as a separate category from "houses". It persisted, almost unquestioned, through all later changes of style, from the London County Council's Neo-Georgian blocks between the wars to the avant-garde work of Denys Lasdun and Goldfinger in the 1950s and 60s (fig 7). What these have in common is their need to affirm their good intentions by emphasising the unity of each development rather than making it connect to surrounding buildings or streets.

The only person I can think of who questioned this was Elizabeth Denby, a housing consultant who was one of the best-informed thinkers and practitioners of housing in Britain in the 1930s (fig 8). In *Europe Rehoused*, 1938, Denby proposed that "all income levels should live within a town, so zoning snobberies should

be abolished, not only for dwellings but for those industries too where their processes are clean and quiet".

In her view, the aesthetic benefits would go hand in hand with the social benefits, for by superseding the long established precedent that blocks of flats should be set back from streets, she believed that her proposal would also "encourage a welcome return to 'street architecture' in Great Britain". So strong, however, was the idea that housing's chief aim was "slum clearance", that the street was seen for years as a danger to health and civic order.

The segregation of social housing has partly been avoided in recent years simply by not building very much of it, and by the political pressure to make every commercial development yield up its tithe of affordable housing. At first, there was a tendency among developers to try and segregate the "affordable" element in order, as they thought, to prevent their commercial housing from being devalued. This short-sighted tactic more often backfired, however, tending to reduce values as well as to contribute stress in daily life. A PTEa-structured scheme such

as Chillingworth Road in Islington, on which PTEa worked with Islington Council, the Guinness Trust, ISHA and a private developer in the late 1990s, was a pioneer in breaking down all the conventional barriers, and proved to be a real portent of the present situation in which the value of houses for sale is high enough to carry the costs of affordable housing and the infrastructure that serves them both (fig 9).

The current PTEa scheme for Arundel Square, also in Islington, is if anything even bolder, since by decking over the cutting of the North London Line, it creates a new amenity for residents in the existing square, which will be completed with a fourth side of mixed-tenure housing on a site that was previously almost unusable (fig 10). The term "social housing" indeed no longer fits when a scheme may involve a mixture of housing for sale (to those able to afford it) and flats for rent, providing the best conditions for a social mix.

In mixed-use schemes PTEa has planned more unusual combinations of housing; for example, with a primary school at St Jude and St Paul's, with children's nurseries at Orsman Road, and with a primary health care centre at Bermondsey Spa. St Jude and St Paul's School offers an instance of PTEa quietly overturning traditional practice. Since schools began, they have usually been distinct and separate from other buildings, not necessarily to the benefit either of the school or of the community. Back in the 1960s, Aldo Rossi demonstrated that functional uses and building "types" were not always the same thing, owing to the exigencies of passing time. Roman remains in Italian cities, for example, were adapted as churches or housing. We have come to realise that this compacting together of different uses is one of the things that makes cities enjoyable, and so the idea of combining a school with housing proves an interesting experiment. The potential for use of school facilities by residents of the flats recovers some of the mild utopianism of Henry Morris's famous Cambridgeshire Village Colleges in the 1930s.

In other schemes, including Crown Wharf Ironworks, on the River Lea, live-work units add to the diversity, fulfilling Denby's call for non-polluting employment integrated with housing in a way she may not have expected. Like building streets, this seems one of those totally obvious historical practices that ceased

Arundel Square proposal by PTEa 2005 (fig 10).

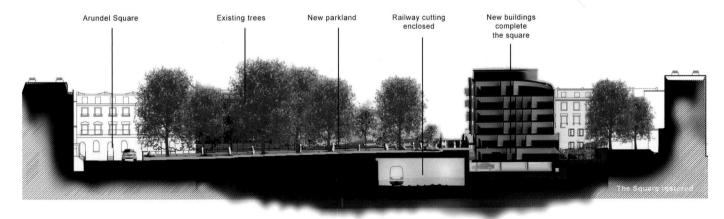

Arundel Square · Existing trees · New parkland · Railway cutting enclosed · New buildings complete the square

23

owing to a misplaced desire to prevent domestic respectability being polluted by the world of work.

In the 1970s and 80s, critics of modern housing saw 'community architecture' as the answer. Ralph Erskine began to meet and listen to the residents at the Byker Estate in Newcastle, which became the image of a new and more friendly form of housing, full of colour and variety, even if still strongly attached to a "heroic" image (fig 11). Then Rod Hackney did his simple refurbishment schemes in Black Road, Macclesfield, which worried the architects because there seemed to be no artistic "signature" in the scheme.

Communities increasingly play a valuable part in early design exercises, and some architects have learnt how to listen to them generously rather than grudgingly. PTEa has brought a spirit of generosity into its community liaison and consultation has become normal practice in their architecture and property developments. It has shown how to use consultation as a way to generate trust, which in turn allowed more imaginative solutions to develop which add value for everyone. Sometimes this can be achieved by a gratuitous good deed, like the scheme to the rear of St Mary's, Islington, where the development paid for the refurbishment of public gardens and repair of the church clock. At a time when local politicians are obliged to behave like narrow-minded business people, architects can show them how to avoid the worst consequences of responsibility without vision.

PTEa's work has mostly been in London; however, there is now a second office in Liverpool and projects are increasingly being undertaken further and further afield. Two

Byker Estate by Ralph Erskine 1980 (fig 11).
photo © Architectural Association Library

significant schemes outside London are included in this volume. One is the work with the Guinness Trust to make the first intervention by a nationally known firm of architects in the highly distinctive shack landscape of Jaywick Sands in Essex, an area rather beloved of architects because the work of amateur "plotland" owner-builders is a form of folk-art architecture. Again, PTEa's tact has worked. The houses it has built in pairs are not overdone. Their board cladding is part of a universal taste of the moment, but at the same time they are enough like the original timber chalets to feel right. In addition, the street layout is quite plain, with just a couple of ponds and a small, paved and tree-planted square adding focus.

The addition of penthouse floors as part of the refurbishment of tower blocks in Sefton Park, the second of these schemes presented here, is something that 15 years ago would have seemed like a bad joke even in this rather leafy part of Liverpool, although equivalent gain in value from development has been practised in London for some time.

What conclusions can one draw from PTEa's body of work? I think there is an analogy with the idea of "paradigm shift" that was proposed by Thomas Kuhn in 1968 as a way of understanding changes in scientific thought. The phrase may have been a little overworked, but it is useful because it indicates how significant changes always gain ground before they are fully recognised. The old paradigm of architecture was based on a hierarchical structure involving architect and client, with the end user and controlling authorities as subsidiaries. The more "heroic" the architecture, the more the end user was taken for granted, while the feelings of the neighbours were simply ignored except on the plane of abstract aesthetic composition. With the re-entry into housing of "exciting" young architects in the last few years, many of them with a particular "look" that serves as their trademark, we risk going backwards into the old paradigm, in which the photographs taken after completion become the chief validation of the scheme.

The alternative that PTEa has been developing over a long time is part of a new paradigm which, while always visually literate and aware, is never over controlled by the need to get a "look", whether Modern or otherwise (fig 12). Although this recent work shows that PTEa has moved closer to modernism, a lot of other things come first, above all people; in the process the old hierarchies have adapted and expanded, like so many structures of modern life, to become networks. This is something that many architectural practices have understood when running their own offices, and now that culture is beginning to be shared by a wider world.

Rethinking

"Significant changes always gain ground before they are fully recognised."

In PTEa's projects, recognising the sequence of events to date for a given site is important groundwork, but the next step often requires an intuitive leap…

Jaywick Sands

A regeneration programme was developed for Jaywick Sands, a seaside community housed in 'plotlands' – dilapidated chalet-style homes. The programme included new infrastructure works, employment and training initiatives and the construction of new homes. PTEa's design of the new houses takes the local timber vernacular and applies innovative construction and energy-conservation techniques.

[BELOW] Urban deprivation and social alienation are not restricted to the inner city. And like in the inner cities the resistance of communities, and their willingness to contribute to change, are the starting points for sustainable renewal.

[ABOVE AND BELOW] The new development facilitates a rolling programme of renovation of original chalets so that the unique character of Jaywick can be safeguarded whilst bringing its basic standards up to respectable current day levels. Site outlined in red below.

[OPPOSITE] An original 'plotlands' dwelling.

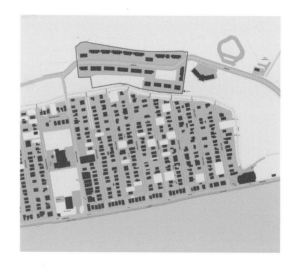

[PREVIOUS PAGE] **PTEa's** 'eco-cabins' extend Jaywick's frontier towards the windswept sand dunes.

[RIGHT, BELOW AND OPPOSITE] The folk-art vernacular of Jaywick Sands 'plotlands' dwellings gave rise to the timber clad aesthetic of PTEa's modest, highly insulated, sustainable modern homes.

Arundel Square

Arundel Square was never completed. After three sides were finished the Victorian developer ran out of money and the North London Line was constructed in a cutting on the south side of the central gardens. Bill Thomas's inspired idea, and the development of his design with PTEa, is a radical proposal to deck over the railway and increase the size of the gardens by 50 per cent. At last, a six storey building completes the square, with a contemporary design of flats with a twin-skin glass facade. The scheme includes the regeneration of the gardens, the restoration of 18 adjacent properties, special needs and affordable housing provision, and a managed garden for biodiversity.

[BELOW AND RIGHT] **The driving through of the North London Line effectively curtailed the completion of the fourth and final side of Arundel Square for over a century.**

Arundel Square

[OPPOSITE] This historic map shows how squares, with central gardens, are an important component in the hierarchy of Islington's urban places.

[RIGHT] The gardens at the heart of the square are enlarged, by half as much again, unfurling them over the railway deck. The square is completed by a modern terrace of 140 flats.

[BELOW] Sectional model of the apartments and the deck over the railway.

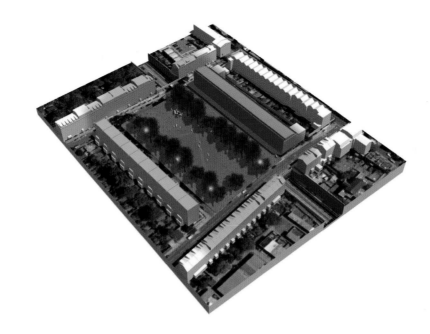

PTEa Precedents

Railway embankments are an interesting and often overlooked resource which on the one hand can be protected as nature reserves or at the other extreme provide development sites. PTEa has long recognised this potential and designed schemes to mitigate the effects of development. At Arundel Square new landscape, a park, was provided by decking over the railway – the undistinguished embankments below were covered up.

In a previous project at Rosemont Road in West Hampstead an inaccessible and overgrown railway embankment was perceived as a nature reserve – but one that could not be entered for study or maintained. PTEa secured a small part of the embankment to create a development opportunity which would renew the street frontage and maintain an urban barrier to the railway. At the same time it created access to the rest of the embankment for essential management, or for study access, while ensuring that it would remain free of development in future.

Where railways pass through on viaducts, rather than in cuttings, the environment is very different – and historically these sites have often been in industrial use. Where the industrial use has declined and urban decay set in these slivers of land can offer up opportunities for regeneration – turning brownfield land back into residential use. Coborn Road in Bow is one such example – creating a tight mews defined on one long side by the railway arches. Lithos Gardens is another, where the landlocked triangle of derelict railway land was brought within an adjacent site to make possible flats, with acoustic measures as a barrier to the railway, and houses and flats around a new communal garden. Several other PTEa schemes preceded the, arguably most daring, idea of overdecking at Arundel Square.

[ABOVE RIGHT] Lithos Gardens, West Hampstead 1996.

[RIGHT] Rosemont Road, West Hampstead 2002.

[OPPOSITE] Arundel Square; the facade of the contemporary apartments is a twin-skin glass one, taking its proportions of clear to opaque glass from the brick pilasters and generous sash windows of the existing terraces around the square. Balconies project through the glass screen into the gardens themselves, like theatre boxes viewing an Arcadian auditorium.

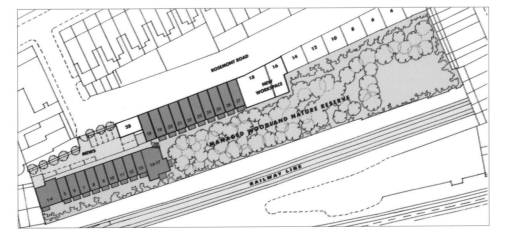

Sefton Park

In the first project to be carried out by PTEa in Liverpool, two tower blocks overlooking the city's renowned Sefton Park have had penthouses added. In addition, a complete refurbishment of the two 15 storey blocks has been carried out including structural repairs, improvements to the common parts, new entrances, landscaping and services, improvements to layouts and the addition of two wheelchair-accessible flats at ground floor level. PTEa has been appointed to proceed to Phase 2 of the project and refurbish a further three blocks.

"The addition of penthouse floors as part of the refurbishment of tower blocks in Sefton Park is something that 15 years ago would have seemed a bad joke, even in this rather leafy part of Liverpool."
ALAN POWERS

"Penthouse" and "towerblock" don't necessarily represent opposite ends of the social spectrum.

St Jude & St Paul's School and Flats

This is a radical prototype to build flats on top of a new primary school. City schools are usually low-rise, occupy a lot of land and are yet undervalued – leaving them vulnerable after school ends and in the long holidays. This project tackles multiple use of land and deals with issues of life-long learning, the need to house teachers in inner London, and security for schools. St Jude & St Paul's School occupied a split site on opposite sides of a road. PTEa and Groveworld joined a site they owned with the school's land next door and designed a new combined infant and junior school on the single site with a three storey block of flats above the classroom wing. The flats will be leased to a housing association; some will be reserved for key-workers including teachers.

[ABOVE] The school with balconies to flats above the classroom wing.

[OPPOSITE] Working model of the school ground floor plan.

[BELOW] The section shows the outward looking flats, and the inward looking school. There is a symbiosis between the two uses, which must complement each other without compromising either. Access arrangements are carefully designed to provide discrete routes, so as to balance informal surveillance with the legitimate concerns of child safety.

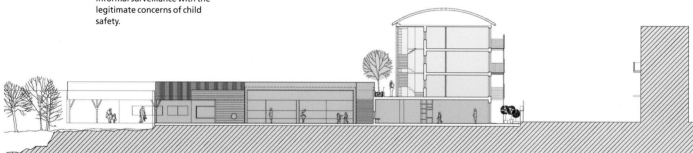

Developers

"The nature of commissions and the way they come to fruition has changed a lot over the years. The client seldom simply walks in with a brief and a site any more."

PTEa's own developments unite design skills and commercial know-how to find the best way of adding value to a particular project. These sites often involve complex planning, technical and legal issues and take several years to assemble into a marketable condition…

Angel Waterside

PTEa won an open competition held by British Waterways in 1998 for the redevelopment of Harris Wharf. The practice was both developer and architect for the mixed-use scheme, Angel Waterside, comprising flats, commercial office space and a landscaped courtyard. Following the competition win a partnership was set up with Groveworld as co-developers. Next to PTEa's base at Diespeker Wharf, the three linked blocks are arranged around a garden courtyard. Each block has a distinctive character; a curved and sloping crystal overhangs the canal; a brick building topped with double-height penthouses looks south over a park and a lower, rendered wing lies on the street with a glazed entrance lodge.

[LEFT] The design relates to four very different contextual conditions around the site.

[RIGHT] To the canal basin, a glass facade reflects the watery landscape and provides panoramic views from the flats. The boat-like form tilts down to the scale of the lockside cottages and creates a stepped garden roofscape.

[OVERLEAF] Angel Waterside is the first phase of regeneration around City Road Basin, following PTEa's masterplan for a linear park all round the dock.

[LEFT] Balconies overlook the park.

[BELOW] PTEa's converted and restored Diespeker Wharf forms the fourth side of the internal courtyard. The terracotta rendered facade of the street wing is kept low to reveal the three distinctive gables of the former timber mill to the street beyond.

Connaught Gardens

This steep, leafy site, in a quiet street near Highgate Wood, was acquired, at auction, by PTEa with a joint venture partner. Set within a residential area of Edwardian terraces and 1960s housing, the proposed row of seven townhouses occupies the footprint of an existing building. With its materials of cedar shingles, render and copper the scheme re-invents the terrace townhouse and plays with the vernacular of the surroundings.

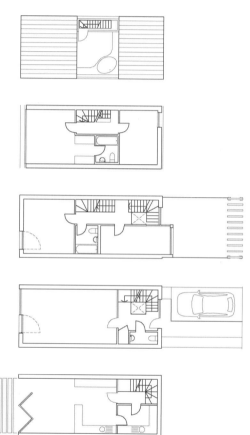

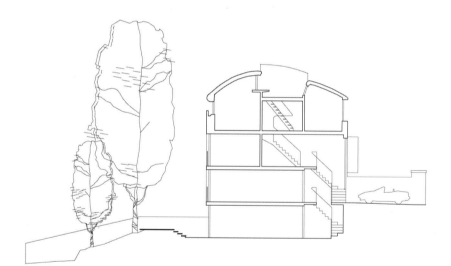

[ABOVE] The typical townhouse section is pulled apart to allow natural light into the centre of the deep plan and expose a secret roof terrace.

[ABOVE RIGHT] The south side of the house is circulation space and a conduit for light and heat; the north side is for long views out and living space.

[OPPOSITE] 'Snapshots' from around the site: each stepped house on the street frontage is individually identified. Cedar shingles cover the garden facade which has long views through mature trees across the valley. The end house turns through 90 degrees to respond to the large houses opposite.

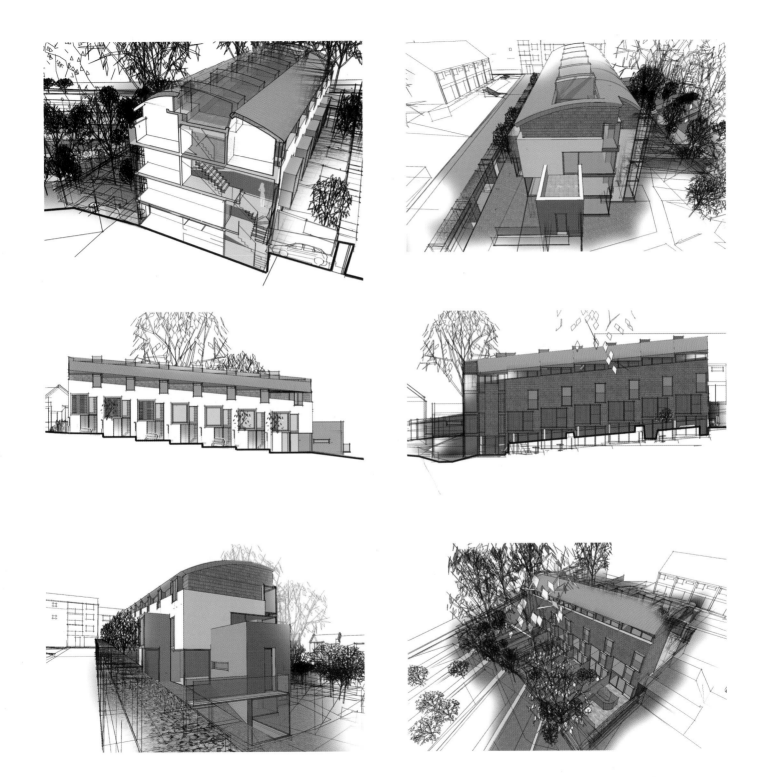

Diespeker Wharf

PTEa completed the restoration and transformation of this listed Victorian timber mill into its office headquarters. A new mezzanine floor hangs from existing trusses, and pyramidal foundations were excavated to increase floor space for offices, conference facilities and residential accommodation. An award-winning garden and landscaped courtyard have been created at the side of the canal and a new two storey timber and glass structure has been added next to the lock. This restoration began the regeneration of the City Road Basin quarter, in Islington, and was followed by two further PTEa projects: Angel Waterside and City Wharf.

[ABOVE] Artist Mat Barber Kennedy's painting of Diespeker Wharf.

[LEFT] Brick, stone, steel, timber and glass: the conversion of a dilapidated mill into prime waterside offices has driven the regeneration of a neglected urban quarter.

[OVERLEAF] PTEa's meeting room opens onto the Regents Canal and the terraces of Islington.

57

PTEa Precedents

When PTEa devised the original Shad Thames masterplan – the catalyst for the Thameside regeneration between Tower Bridge and what is now the Design Museum – loft living was an idea still confined to the artistic neighbourhoods of New York. In England, former wharfs and warehouses were still the shells of Blake's Satanic mills, and as likely to be demolished as turned into expensive apartments.

New Concordia Wharf, an imposing building on a muddy tidal creek, set a standard in high quality restoration and conversion. This blueprint of retaining, but not over-restoring existing fabric – visibly mending, while adding appropriate sympathetic new material – has informed a string of PTEa projects.

This is in contrast to what David Chipperfield has called the "caricature" of asserting aggressive modern infill with an over-heightened approach to showcasing historic structure.

At the Anchor Brewhouse, PTEa converted the former Courage Brewery into residential use. Intact parts, such as the boilerhouse, were restored with unobtrusive new openings and additions. The bomb-damaged brewhouse was infilled with a modern steel and glass structure, but one whose design was modelled on the former timber-boarded facades of the brewery discovered by research into archive material and old photographs.

PTEa followed a similar approach when tackling its own building at Diespeker, with the additional constraints of carrying out the work in several phases with the architectural practice in occupation.

[ABOVE RIGHT] Anchor Brewhouse, Shad Thames 1991.

[RIGHT] New Concordia Wharf, Southwark 1983.

[OPPOSITE] PTEa respects the marks of age, touching the existing fabric as lightly as possible and ensuring modern insertions such as sliding glass doors and mezzanine stairs are complementary.

City Wharf

With Angel Waterside nearing completion, PTEa and Groveworld initiated a second phase of their masterplan for City Road Basin. Overlooking the linear park and the basin is a high-density, multi-tenure residential scheme of flats for sale and affordable housing. The scheme forms a tight urban streetscape to Graham Street which frees up at high level to create a rooftop landscape of penthouses and gardens with views over the canal basin and to the City of London.

[BELOW LEFT AND RIGHT]
Developing the street facade: the long elevation is divided into blocks by projecting bays and balconies allowing views up and down the street and bringing in sunlight. Privacy screens are overlayed allowing individual expression of the blocks. Rooftop penthouses are set back from the street.

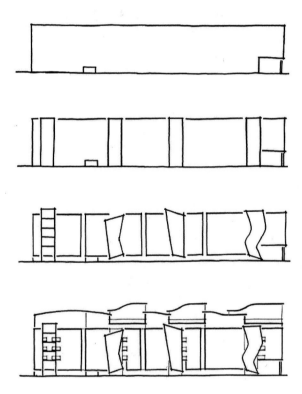

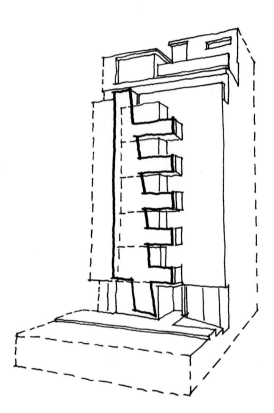

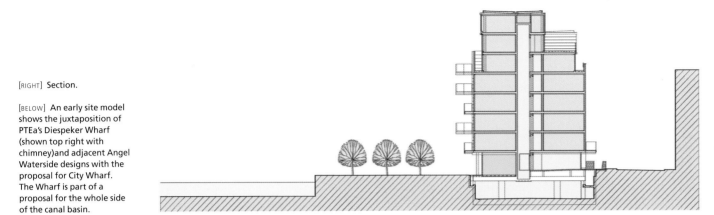

[RIGHT] Section.

[BELOW] An early site model shows the juxtaposition of PTEa's Diespeker Wharf (shown top right with chimney)and adjacent Angel Waterside designs with the proposal for City Wharf. The Wharf is part of a proposal for the whole side of the canal basin.

[OVERLEAF] Elevations.

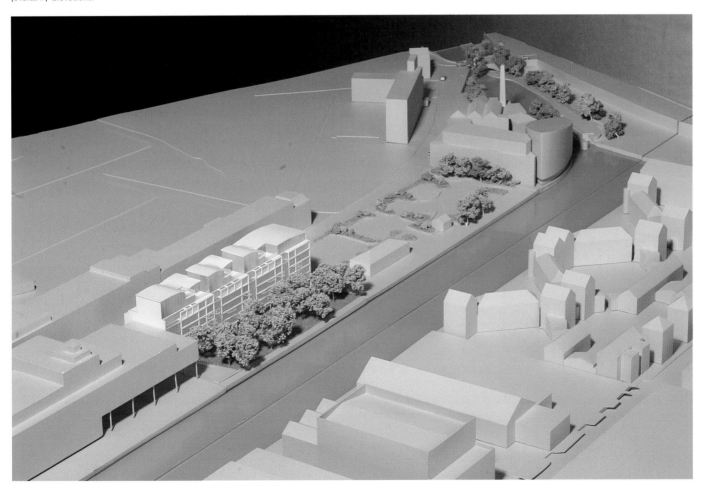

Community

"PTEa has brought a spirit of generosity into its community liaison and consultation has become normal practice in its architecture and property developments."

Consultation determines the requirements and aspirations of user groups. It is important to extend the definition of client to the immediate neighbours and general public…

Whitechapel Community Sports Centre

Whitechapel Community Sports Centre was designed to encourage all members of the neighbourhood, even those normally put off by the usual ambiance of sports centres, to participate. After a widespread consultation PTEa designed a friendly and welcoming building that appeals to members of the local Asian community, especially women, as well as being accessible to people with disabilities. Special needs have been discreetly and efficiently accommodated in the centre, which comprises a women-only fitness area, an all-weather pitch, general fitness and training provision, a multi-purpose hall and social areas, including a cafe and a crêche. The centre's glass enclosed café provides a social meeting space for the community, as well as sports users.

[OPPOSITE] The entrance facade of warm brick curves to embrace a proposed urban plaza.

[ABOVE] The community sports centre's oversailing gymnasia roofs glimpsed from Whitechapel Road.

Hang glider trusses articulate
the admission of roof lighting
into different gymnasia which
open off the internal street.

[ABOVE] Young footballers from Whitechapel's multi-ethnic community.

[LEFT] The "internal street" connects the entrance and cafe with a succession of discrete or linked activity rooms, outdoor pitches and gardens.

Brockwell Park Lido

Brockwell Park Lido, in Herne Hill, south London, was built in 1937 in Art Deco/proto-Modernist style. It was listed Grade II in 2003. For the next 25 years it will be run by Fusion, a not-for-profit leisure company, on behalf of Lambeth Council and local people. The task is to refurbish and extend the lido to allow it to become financially self-sufficient. Spaces include a gymnasium, dance studios, yoga rooms, a crèche and a spa. The lido commands great local affection and the project has involved much community consultation. The challenge is to rejuvenate the Lido without losing the fabulous atmosphere that makes it such a well-loved place (its other name is "Brixton beach").

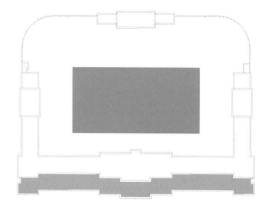

[ABOVE] Brockwell Park Lido has two "fronts" – an inside and an outside one. The existing accommodation is very shallow – effectively an occupied wall, enclosing the pool and sunbathing decks. This design "re-constructs" the park-side elevation (actually a new-build, shown in grey, with subtle changes to fenestration) about six metres further out, creating a deep usable space within.

[OPPOSITE] Heavenly bodies – hand-tinted Lido scene from the golden age.

Grahame Park

High-density housing is not always restricted to the inner city. At Grahame Park, designing jointly with Levitt Bernstein Associates, PTEa are working to regenerate the Grahame Park Estate and the wider surrounding area, developing a framework for high-density housing in a suburban context. Over 3,000 new homes will be provided, arranged in neighbourhoods each with its own identity. The urban grain of streets will be introduced.

[OPPOSITE] PTEa's masterplan aims to re-urbanise the area, providing a street pattern of clear routes, open spaces with defined uses and housing densification. The result will be a mixed-tenure neighbourhood of private housing, key-worker and shared-ownership homes and affordable rented housing.

[ABOVE] The contrasts of this pocket of suburbia: potentially lovely natural environment, set against the social isolation of difficult-to-manage post-war housing complexes.

[RIGHT] PTEa's completed Adastral Phase 1 is a prototype for the much larger Grahame Park neighbourhood.

[ABOVE LEFT] The masterplan process scrutinises all aspects of design. A permeability analysis compares existing and proposed routes. This layout shows routes through the existing neighbourhood, Colindale North.

[LEFT] A comparison is made with the existing estate layout. Underpasses, blind alleyways and cul-de-sacs, allow poor visual connections and plentiful escape routes for those considering crime.

[BELOW LEFT] The proposal replaces the layout with a wider choice of alternative through routes and greater visual permeability.

[ABOVE] Masterplanning of new neighbourhoods is PTEa's deepest engagement with communities. The practice strives to include even sceptical and alienated groups to produce a unified vision.

PTEa Precedents

The redevelopment of a large neighbourhood, involving hundreds or thousands of people, is a very different problem to that of infilling a gap in an existing townscape. A framework for development that embraces spatial hierarchies, transport networks and design codes needs to have its own identity. Nevertheless, except in a genuine greenfield setting there are likely to be existing patterns in the surrounding area and underlying patterns beneath the tabula rasa of British post war planning.

Two previous PTEa projects attempted to knit together the very different patterns of modernist estate planning (island blocks around ill-defined green space, backs facing fronts, segregated or split-level pedestrian routes) with Victorian streets.

In the Peckham Partnership regeneration, designed with BPTW architects, new streets form links through to adjoining cul-de-sacs – creating clear through-routes but avoiding car rat-runs. Formally, the language of brick together with modernist use of steel balconies and glass blocks resonates with its more brutalist neighbours in refurbished "Unité"-style slabs.

At Lefevre Walk, in Bow, the demolition of the existing estate was the preferred outcome of intensive discussions with the existing residents. The former abrupt disjunction between the rejuvenated area from artist Rachel Whiteread's *House* along Roman Road to the Blackwall Tunnel Approach has now been restructured to form a pedestrian-friendly, ground-level quarter. This is bounded by a barrier block that mitigates the effect of the motorway on the eastern edge.

[ABOVE RIGHT] Gloucester Grove, Peckham 2001.

[RIGHT] Lefevre Walk, Bow 2003.

Repairing the city fabric: some guidelines

Edward Woods neighbourhood

BY BILL THOMAS

"The aim of city housing work is to integrate new fabric and hence new households into the existing matrix/organisation of the city. It is also to create urban places, structures and events which add to the enjoyment of the public realm."

Architects' Journal, 30 May 1996

[OPPOSITE] City housing has been blighted by both the demolition of serviceable traditional stock and the failures of post war estate design. Now it is necessary to mend both.
photo © Getty Images

This checklist is abridged from Bill Thomas's paper published in the *Architects' Journal* in May 1996. Its topic is inserting appropriate new housing into urban areas – a complex and sensitive process which requires painstaking research.

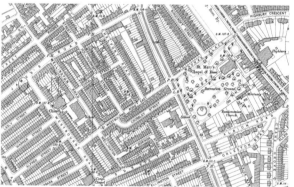

1 [ABOVE] Edward Woods Estate, before – disparate scales of buildings separated by concrete and tarmac.

2 [LEFT] Historic maps suggest underlying patterns.

3 [BELOW] Edward Woods neighbourhood design evolution – old and new buildings are integrated around a new landscaped garden.

An integral objective of bringing new work into place is completing or mending broken, unfinished or amputated bits of town. The whole neighbourhood can be greater than the parts by enhancing and collaborating with the existing surroundings. It is also important to graft the needs of the future and the latest technology onto the existing context.

1   Understand and work within the anatomy of the urban surroundings.

2   Examine the existing fabric: starting with the Ordnance Survey, look hard at the patterns which surround the site and go back through the available historic maps, overlaying them on the project site and its surroundings.

3   Insert contemporary accommodation that is compatible with what is already there. Looking at a map of the evolution of a condition helps to predict (and shape) the next stage in that evolution.

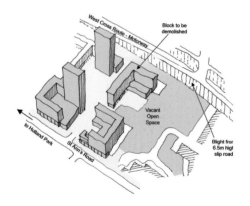

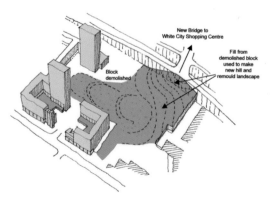

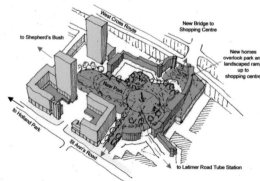

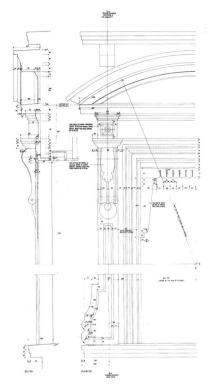

4   Take lots of photographs of the surroundings of the site, and get copies of historic photos in order to build up a 3-D textural picture of the neighbourhood.

5   Commission detailed geometrical surveys, including 3-D details of features of neighbouring sites and buildings.

6   Embrace help from anyone who cares to offer it (for example, neighbours, interest groups, the council, possible future residents).

7   Introduce yourselves to those who you are about to inconvenience – write to all the neighbours and inform them of your intentions and invite them to come and give their views. These neighbours will provide a great deal of useful knowledge and will generally be willing to share it with you.

4 [ABOVE] Archive images help to understand the history of the neighbourhood.

5 [ABOVE RIGHT] Measured drawings provide accurate information about surrounding details.

6 [RIGHT] Open days encourage neighbours to get involved.

7 [RIGHT BELOW] Newsletters keep people informed and draw out useful information and comment.

8 [ABOVE] **Making contact with local VIPs.**

9 [ABOVE RIGHT] **Parties are a good way to get the consultation process going.**

10 [BELOW] **Stitching in even the smallest repairs adds enjoyment and value.**

8 Involve the local authority early in the process and recognise the contribution it can make – use the planner's database, knowledge and opinions.

9 Where available, engage the end users of a design. To find out what the future users of buildings would really like, organise:

- parties (at the start, middle and completion of the design)
- coach trips (to similar projects)
- a series of residents' design meetings
- regular surgeries along with the design committee meetings
- special meetings targeting particular interest groups
- participatory exhibitions
- regular newsletters
- permanent 'shop windows'.

10 Well-serviced city land is a precious resource – don't waste any. Don't leave any funny little triangular or wedge-shaped bits of wasted ground. The cost of a party-wall award, for example, is generally trivial compared with the extra value obtained by closing and using the gap. Equally importantly, the result helps create an appropriate urban form.

Finally, further research: the techniques outlined here are woefully inadequate when set against some of the larger problems beginning to surface. For such problems we don't need prophecy, experiment or a new vision; we need information, observation technique and research. Other areas of work which would generate useful tools include:

- Measuring how the number of householders sharing a secured entrance affects quality and manageability
- The real housing-management costs of built-form decisions

- Objective validation of some "design rules" which PTEa use but can't always prove, such as the minimisation of common parts in family housing
- Measuring urban permeability and its consequences in residential areas of different kinds
- The use and effect of urban gates.

Relatively tiny amounts of money spent on researching these and other design questions would help to ensure that this time urban housing is sustainable.

[BELOW] Edward Woods complete – regenerated, sustainable, mixed-tenure, high-density housing on brownfield land.

Modernity

"In its sensitivity to various kinds of London typology, PTEa can claim the most respectable Modernist ancestry."

What is traditional is not, necessarily, opposed to what is Modern...

Terracotta Court & Park West Apartments

These two adjacent residential buildings in Bermondsey have very different outlooks. One faces onto the busy Tower Bridge Road and is clad in terracotta tiles on a prefabricated inner leaf construction. The other overlooks a park and is more informally elevated in brick, timber and glass. The external materials were selected to engage with the surrounding palette, with the glazed elements elegantly linking the new with the old.

The building completes a row of Victorian warehouses – the living space windows reflect the proportions of the adjacent loading bays and are angled to provide views of Tower Bridge. The bedroom windows are punched holes within the terracotta facade – a modern interpretation of the red brick surroundings.

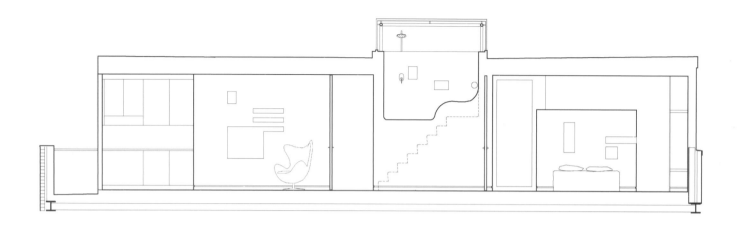

[TOP] The raised shower-room of the penthouse in the Park West Apartments gives views over central London.

[ABOVE] Niches within the interior provide storage, display and natural lighting.

[LEFT] The apartments overlooking Tanner Street Park.

[OPPOSITE] Sometimes the context of architecture is the panorama of the urban skyline. Here a minimally enclosed contemporary space has been created and the boundary is the curtain of the urban fabric itself.

Crown Wharf Ironworks

Crown Wharf Ironworks, a riverside development in east London on the edge of the proposed Olympic Village, is the first in a series of mixed-use developments that will transform a derelict industrial site into a vibrant commercial and residential complex. The old forge building will be restored to house a museum, café and live-work units. PTEa co-owned this site and established the new planning use before selling-on, continuing as architects.

Joseph Bazalgette's heroic Northern Outfall Sewer frames the view of romantic dilapidation at Crown Wharf, Fish Island, on the River Lea Navigation.

[LEFT] The crisp white forms of two new live-work blocks are set back from the river to create an open courtyard, centered on the forge, with spectacular views across the River Lea.

[RIGHT] Old Forge interior to be converted into a museum and cafe.

[BELOW] The site is at the junction of the river and a linear park – The Green Way.

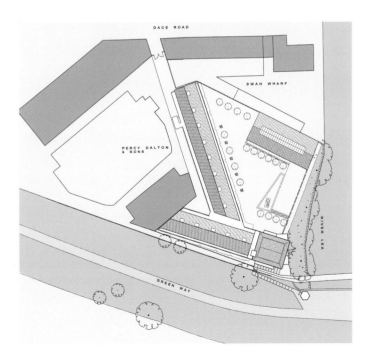

Chillingworth Road

Chillingworth Road is a mixed-tenure housing scheme of private for sale homes, shared ownership flats and affordable housing with a communal play area and parking. The Government White Paper "Our Towns & Cities. The Future: Delivering an Urban Renaissance" commended Chillingworth Road:

"This is a convincing demonstration that skilled designers, working closely with supportive clients and local planning officers, can produce housing of an appropriate urban scale and type for an integrated mix of tenures and household sizes. High standards of design, construction and planning mean that this development should be a social as well as a commercial success."

[RIGHT] The Modernist use of glass blocks promotes light and security close to the street.

[BOTTOM LEFT] In the spirit of Bruno Taut, or of Goldfinger's Willow Road, Chillingworth Road's modern brick elevations respect the street tradition. Behind the facades residents range from renting students to large family owner-occupiers; much like any typical north London street.

[LEFT] Site plan – the terraces wrap around communal gardens and parking.

[BELOW] Careful composition using a limited palette of good quality materials designed for longevity in a tough part of the city.

PTEa Precedents

In the 1980s and 90s PTEa completed modest precedents for Chillingworth Road, in which a diverse mix of unit sizes, of flats and homes and of affordable rented or owner-occupied homes were assembled behind a unifying facade that drew inspiration from the ordinary London building stock around.

The expression of different income levels was repressed in order to avoid stigmatising the recipients of state-subsidised housing and to recognise that as Peter Ackroyd says "everything connects".

Small flat blocks mimic the scale of Georgian houses – although the expression of the flat type is played down, in fact all those Georgian houses are now actually small blocks of flats. At Wren Street and Gough Street the stripped, almost austere, facades slot into Georgian Bloomsbury – adopting the mews precedent.

At Draper Place, two of the oldest houses in Islington were renovated and incorporated in a new urban cloister. The colonnaded ground floor unifies a variety of houses and flats whose understated expression only breaks out on the rear facades which face onto a council estate and a churchyard respectively. Stone from another of PTEa's sites – a demolished stoneyard – enhances the simple brick facades to the square, while the spaces have tidying-up works and boundary improvements (even the restoring of the church clock) as a consequence of PTEa "looking beyond the immediate site".

[ABOVE RIGHT] Gough Street, Bloomsbury 1991.

[RIGHT] Draper Place, Islington 1994.

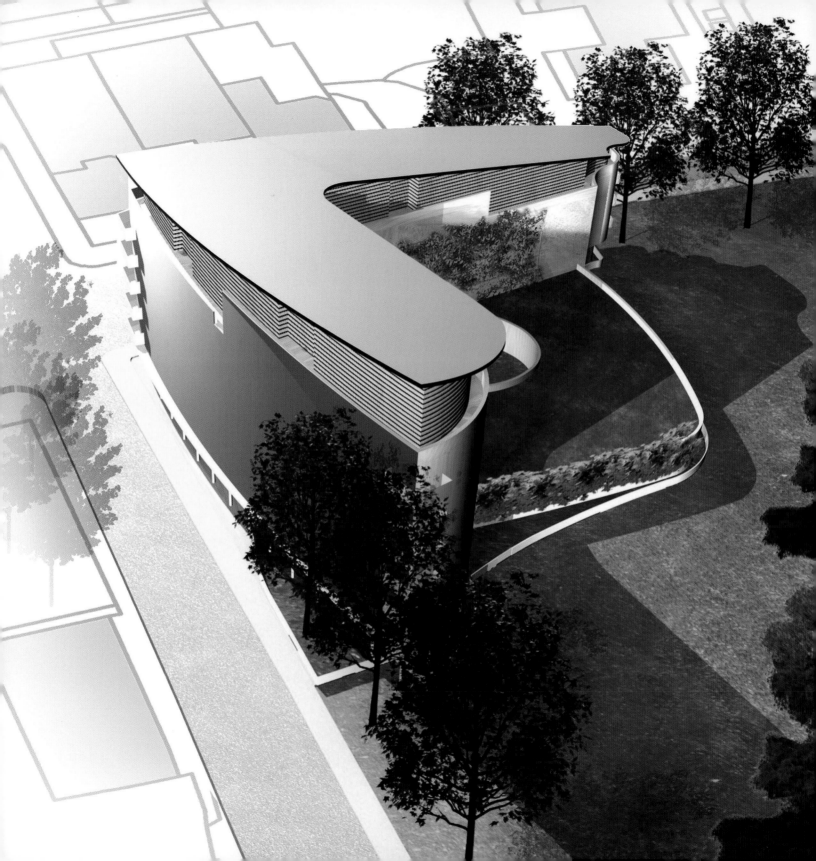

Spa Central

Spa Central is part of the Bermondsey Spa Regeneration initiative and is designed in collaboration with Dransfield Owens de Silva. It combines neighbourhood resources with a sustainable living environment. The ground floor is dedicated to community uses; a health centre includes a dentist, pharmacy and nursery. Space above provides mixed-tenure accommodation: affordable, key-worker and private homes for sale. Environmental and sustainability issues are key to the scheme, which incorporates water from a borehole (a new spa for Bermondsey), combined heat and power and a car club available for residents' use.

[TOP AND OPPOSITE] The 'green banana' was a competition-winning design which proposed a crescent of flats enclosing the edge of a park. It included a range of sustainable initiatives and a 'green' roof over the single storey health centre.

[ABOVE AND RIGHT] The zinc facade of overlapping and stepped slot windows flows around the perimeter sweep of the park – creating a distinctive new identity in a nondescript area of London. Unusually for PTEa this is designed to be a landmark, to initiate and symbolise the Bermondsey Spa regeneration masterplan.

Belvedere Court

This pioneering high density regeneration scheme marks the transformation of a rundown corner of Hackney from a neglected brownfield site to a twenty-first century urban space. The site is close to Regents Canal and burgeoning live-work units around Kingsland Basin and is the first major affordable housing project in an area undergoing large-scale urban renewal.

The seven storey apartment block mixes homes for affordable rent and shared ownership. The scheme was designed so that the classes of tenure would be hard to tell apart. What appears to be one block is in fact three self-contained blocks with separate entrances.

[ABOVE] **Neighbouring buildings.**

[LEFT AND OPPOSITE] **Utilising brownfield land on the fringe of an austere post war council estate, Belvedere Court adds a dash of colour in a direct, contemporary way, sympathetic to its Modernist neighbours.**

Chronology: selected past work

1974 Vandyke Works

1975 The Tileries

1976 Colebrooke Row Offices

1977 Woodbridge Estate

1982 Norland Road

1983 New Concordia Wharf

1984 Tower & York Houses

1985 Frestonia Community Project

1978 Clarence Estate

1979 Leybourne Street

1980 Fitzjohns Avenue

1981 Eldon Grove

1986 De Barowe Mews

1987 Knightsmead Special School

1988 Becklow Mews

1989 Goldhawk Road

1990 Southam Street Workshops   1991 Anchor Brewhouse   1992 Old Royal Free Square   1993 Wiltshire Road

1998 Canham Mews TV Studios   1999 Mountford House   2000 Doves Yard   2001 St Luke's Church Hall

1994 SCPR Offices

1995 Haverstock Hill

1996 Lithos Road

1997 Clapton Park

2002 Delta House

2003 Butler's Yard

2004 Naish Court

2005 Adastral South

Selected Bibliography

PETER ACKROYD
Blake
Minerva, 1996

PETER ARNELL
AND TED BICKFORD
Aldo Rossi Buildings and Projects
Rizzoli, 1985

GASTON BACHELARD
The Poetics of Space
Translated by Maria Jolas.
Orion Press, 1964

JORGE LUIS BORGES
The Total Library
Allen Lane, 2000

M CHRISTINE BOYER
The City of Collective Memory
MIT Press, 1994

MARK BUCHANAN
Ubiquity
The Science of history … or why the
world is simpler than we think
Phoenix, 2001

GORDON CULLEN
Concise Townscape
Architectural Press, 1994

ANDRES DUANY AND
ELIZABETH PLATER-ZYBERCK
Towns and Townmaking Principles
Rizzoli, 1991

ANDREW DUNCAN
Secret London (Globetrotter
Walking Guides)
New Holland, 2003

LIONEL ESHER
A Broken Wave
Penguin, 1981

ROBIN EVANS
Figures , Doors & Passageways,
1978
in AA Documents 2, 1997

ALEC FORSHAW
20th Century Buildings in Islington
Islington Society, 2001

HERBERT GIRARDET
Creating Sustainable Cities
Green Books, 1999

MARK GIROUARD
Life in the English Country House
Yale, 1978

STEVEN GROAK
The Idea of Building
E & FN Spon, 1992

JASON HAWKES
AND FELIX BARKER
London from the Air
Ebury Press, 2001

MARK HAWORTH-BOOTH (Editor)
The Street Photographs of
Roger Mayne
Victoria & Albert Museum, 1986

BILL HILLIER
AND JULIENNE HANSON
The Social Logic of Space
Cambridge University Press, 1984

RUSSELL HOBAN
Amaryllis Night and Day
Bloomsbury, 2001

J B JACKSON
The Necessity for Ruins
The University of Massachusetts
Press, 1980

ANTHONY JACKSON
The Politics of Architecture
Architectural Press, 1970

JANE JACOBS
Death and Life of the Great
American Cities
Random House, 1993

STEVEN JOHNSON
Emergence
Scribner, 2002

PETER KATZ
The New Urbanism: Toward an
Architecture of Community
McGraw-Hill, 1993

ROBERT MAXWELL
Sweet Disorder and the Carefully
Careless
Princetown Papers on Architecture,
1993

ROY PORTER
London, A Social History
Penguin, 1994

STEEN EILER RASMUSSEN
London the Unique City
Pelican, 1961

RILEY AND BERGDOLL
Mies in Berlin
MOMA, 2001

DAVID RUDLIN
AND NICHOLAS FALK
Building the 21st century Home
(the sustainable urban
neighbourhood)
Architectural Press, 1998

CHRISTIAN SCHITTICH (editor)
' High Density Housing' Concepts –
Planning – Construction
Birkhauser, nd

RICHARD SENNETT
The Fall of Public Man
WW Norton, 1992

IAIN SINCLAIR
Lights Out for the Territory
Granta, 1997

ZADIE SMITH
White Teeth
Penguin, 2001

GRAHAM SWIFT
Last Orders
Picador, 1996

JUN'ICHIRO TANIZAKI
In Praise of Shadows
Vintage, 2001

FRANCIS TIBBALDS
Making People-Friendly Towns
Spon Press, 2000

RICHARD TRENCH,
AND ELLIS HILLMAN
London Under London
John Murray, 1993

CRAIG WHITAKER
Architecture of the American
Dream
Three Rivers Press, 1998

TOM WOLFE
From Bauhaus to Our House
Jonathan Cape, 1981

Project data

Rethinking

Jaywick Sands
nr Clacton, Essex CO5

COMPLETION	2002
NO. OF HOMES	40 new homes
VALUE	Phase 1: £2.5m
CLIENT	The Guinness Trust
AWARDS	RIBA Housing Design Award 1999
	Civic Trust Special Award for Rural Housing 2001
	RIBA Housing Design Award (Completed Building) 2001

Arundel Square
Islington, London N1

COMPLETION	2008
VALUE	£26m
CLIENT	Bill Thomas and New Islington & Hackney Housing Association
AWARDS	RIBA Housing Design Award 2004

Sefton Park
Liverpool, L17

COMPLETION	Phase 1 2003
NO. OF HOMES	Phase 1: 112 flats
VALUE	Phase 1: £15m
CLIENT	Liverpool Housing Action Trust
AWARDS	Civic Trust Partnership Award 2004

St Jude & St Paul's CE School
Islington, London N1

COMPLETION	Easter 2005
NO. OF HOMES	24 flats
VALUE	£4m
CLIENT	Harris Wharf Development Co Ltd (a joint venture between PTE Services and Groveworld), London Diocesan Board for Schools, Islington & Shoreditch Housing Association

Developers

Angel Waterside
Islington, London N1

COMPLETION	November 2003
NO. OF HOMES	57 apartments for sale + commercial space
VALUE	£9m
CLIENT	Harris Wharf Development Co Ltd (a joint venture between PTE Services and Groveworld)
AWARDS	National Homebuilder Design Awards: Best Use of a Brownfield Site 2004.
	Your New Home Awards: Best Waterside Development and Highly Commended for Best Exterior Design 2004

Connaught Gardens
Muswell Hill, London N10

COMPLETION	Spring 2007
NO. OF HOMES	7 terraced houses
VALUE	£4m
CLIENT	Connaught House Developments Ltd (a joint venture between PTE Property (Connaught) Ltd and Guild Developments)

Diespeker Wharf
Islington, London N1

COMPLETION	1999
VALUE	£600,000
CLIENT	Diespeker Holdings
AWARDS	Civic Trust Commendation for Landscaping 2000
	Islington Society Award: Highly Commended 1997

City Wharf
Islington, London N1

COMPLETION	Spring 2007
NO. OF HOMES	83 mixed tenure homes + commercial space
VALUE	£12.5m
CLIENT	City Wharf Development Co Ltd (a joint venture between PTE Services and Groveworld Ltd)

Community

Whitechapel Community Sports Centre
Bethnal Green, London E1

COMPLETION	1998
VALUE	£3m
CLIENT	London Borough of Tower Hamlets/Bethnal Green City Challenge Ltd
AWARDS	Reds Awards: Best Public Sports and Leisure Centre/Pool, 2002

Brockwell Park Lido
Herne Hill, London SE24

COMPLETION	October 2005
VALUE	£1.9m
CLIENT	Fusion Lifestyle

Grahame Park
Barnet, London NW9

COMPLETION	2002–2015
NO. OF HOMES	over 3,000 new homes + comprehensive amenities and facilities
VALUE	£350m
CLIENT	Choices for Grahame Park (London Borough of Barnet, Notting Hill Housing Trust, Genesis Housing Trust)

Repairing the city fabric:
Edward Woods neighbourhood
Shepherds Bush, London W11

COMPLETION	2003
NO. OF HOMES	122 new homes
VALUE	£13m
CLIENT	Notting Hill Housing Trust and Countryside in Partnership
AWARDS	'What House' Award Best Partnership Scheme 2003
	National Homebuilders Awards: Best Partnership Development 2003

Modernity

Terracotta Court & Park West Apartments
Southwark, London SE1

COMPLETION	2001
NO. OF HOMES	27 flats + offices
VALUE	£4.5m
CLIENT	Rooff Residential

Crown Wharf Ironworks
Fish Island, Bow, London E3

COMPLETION	April 2005
NO. OF HOMES	77 live-work units
VALUE	£8.5m
CLIENT	Planning: PTE Property and Frank Luke. Development: LondonGreen Developments Ltd

Chillingworth Road
Islington, London N1

COMPLETION	2001
NO. OF HOMES	67 mixed tenure homes
VALUE	£4.5m
CLIENT	Galliard Homes, The Guinness Trust, Islington and Shoreditch Housing Association
AWARDS	Britannia National Homebuilder Awards: Commendation for Best Use of Brownfield Site 2001

Spa Central
Bermondsey, London SE16

COMPLETION	February 2007
NO. OF HOMES	73 new homes
VALUE	£10m
CLIENT	Rooff Residential, PTE Property and Hyde Housing Association

Belvedere Court
Hackney, London N1

COMPLETION	2004
NO. OF HOMES	72 new homes
VALUE	£6.7m
CLIENT	Islington & Shoreditch Housing Association

PTEa Practice

Pollard Thomas Edwards architects (PTEa) is in the vanguard of architect-led, socially responsible property development and has more than 30 years' experience of both the public and private sectors. Targeting neglected inner-city sites where mainstream developers see too much risk, it has united design skills and business acumen to produce many commercially successful schemes which have also won awards for urban design and architectural quality. It also pursues joint ventures and is heavily committed to community participation in its endeavours. The practice is equally comfortable tackling huge projects – creating a new town for 10,000 people or reshaping whole neighbourhoods – as it is designing smaller, bespoke buildings such as sports halls, schools or a TV studio. In all projects PTEa aims to make our towns and cities better places to live.

The practice operates from its own canalside offices in Islington, London, which provide a stimulating and dynamic environment for its staff and visitors. The successful combination of creative informality and efficient business systems evident at Diespeker Wharf is reflected in the broad approach PTEa takes to projects. The practice recently opened an office in Liverpool, which has already added a Civic Trust award to the tally of over 50 major design awards won by the London office.

PTEa was founded by Roger Pollard, Bill Thomas and John Edwards. It is now a private limited company owned by seven working directors. The majority shareholders Andrew Beharrell, Teresa Borsuk, Stephen Chance and Stephen Fisher lead on strategy. Dominic May directs office management and operations together with Judith Marshall and Ben Scantlebury ,the systems manager. Andrew Humpherson is currently managing PTEa Liverpool. The practice is committed to a wide degree of collaboration and devolution amongst its associates, administrative and technical staff.

The practice has built up long standing relationships with clients, key consultants, and individuals, far too many to name here, but we would like to thank everyone for their commitment to PTEa over many years.

PTEa is an equal opportunities employer, with an equal split of male and female staff. It employs people from many countries and 23 languages are spoken within the office.

Current staff:

DIRECTORS: Andrew Beharrell, Teresa Borsuk, Stephen Chance, Stephen Fisher, Andrew Humpherson, Judith Marshall, Dominic May.

ASSOCIATES: Chris Bills, Lee Davies, Sarah Eastham, David Graham, Harry Hamberger, Roger Holdsworth, Rachel Livings, Nick Macarthur, Mike O'Rourke, Patricia Patel, Robin Saha-Choudhury, Ben Scantlebury, Carl Vann.

Hershey Ansay, Anna Bamber, Arun Baybars, Mark Bennett, Amanda Bisley, Kaye Bogues, Roger Borland, Jitesh Brahmkshatnya, Cathy Buckley, Alexis Butterfield, Albert Chan, Ming Cheng, Khisha Clarke, Giuseppe Clienti, Aron Coates, Martin Craig, Patrick Devlin, Elizabeth Dow, Jan Dunsmuir, Ursula Eady, Wendy Ebringer, Jo Edwards, Sarrah El-Bushra, Daniel Fennings, Jean Franco, Frazer Gardiner, Francesca Gernone, Katie Huggins, Joel Iseli, Matthew James, Ling Jiang, Jeng Jyh, Scott Kelly, Wolfgang Kuchler, Mona Kvanka, Theo Lall, Philip Lee, Patrick LeLarge, Min Li, Guilherme Lopes, Angels Lopez, Katrin Lotz, Peter Lunter, Mhairi McVicar, Peggy Mead, Megumi Nagai, Marly Nicolaou, Dominique Oliver, Leo Pollock, Peter Prescott, Patricia Lozano Quintana, Sarah Ransome, Helen Reay, Adriaan Rensen, Gianni Rocchi, Jamie Scantlebury, Mary Sefton, Andrew Stokes, Tammy Storey, Tristan Stout, Mark Sustr, Scott Theobold, Bronwen Thomas, Lucy Thomas, Marcela Thornton-Jones, Emma Toogood, Hoi Yat Tsoi, Catherine van der Loos, Kishor Vekaria, Isabel Vicens, Emma Williams, Greg Wilson, Kate Wong, John Yeudall, Robert Young.

Every Thursday it is someone's turn to cook lunch for the whole office to eat together.